T0158946

"IT'S HERE"

"IT'S HERE"

WRITTEN AND ILLUSTRATED BY

JUNE M. LAWRENCE

iUniverse LLC
Bloomington

"IT'S HERE"

This publication is nonfiction. The names have been changed to protect the living.

iUniverse books may be ordered through booksellers or by contacting:

iUniverse LLC
1663 Liberty Drive
Bloomington, IN 47403
www.iuniverse.com
1-800-Authors (1-800-288-4677)

Because of the dynamic nature of the Internet, any web addresses or links contained in this book may have changed since publication and may no longer be valid. The views expressed in this work are solely those of the author and do not necessarily reflect the views of the publisher, and the publisher hereby disclaims any responsibility for them.

The illustrations provided are solely those of the author June M. Lawrence and depict only herself.

ISBN: 978-1-4917-0230-7 (sc)
ISBN: 978-1-4917-0231-4 (ebk)

Printed in the United States of America

iUniverse rev. date: 08/02/2013

Dedication

It took me a period of many years to muster up enough courage to write this book. It took me less than two weeks to write it, after I did.

After all, I already knew the story. All I had to do was put it on paper.

The hard part was reliving it.

This book is not a work of fiction. All of the stories actually happened during the many years that I lived in that house

I dedicate this book to my darling husband, for always believing in me and for encouraging me to share these experiences with others.

He is the reason I was there in the first place, and he's the reason I stayed.

Acknowledgements

I wish to sincerely thank all of my family and friends who encouraged me to finish this book. It took a lot of courage to relive all of those experiences but without those individuals and those that were part of the experience, my undying gratitude.

Without those that shared those experiences, it would have been just me that would have been relating the stories, which would then be open to skepticism. The names have been changed to protect those of the living.

Probably the most skeptical was my husband—until the odor hit him. Now he knows!

June had also written "Seasons of Love, Laughter and Sorrow" in paperback from iUniverse.

Preface

Perhaps you've seen this place.

Driving by on the highway adjacent to us, it can be seen looming in the background behind two large fields.

Or possibly you were one of the curiosity seekers that just wanted to see what was at the end of the posted, dead end road. You might even have been one of the avid hunters requesting permission to hunt this land that is so prevalent with deer. It's even possible you might have been one of the people that snuck past our house after dark, into the wooded section.

No matter which of these categories you fit in, it would have been virtually impossible not to notice the house.

Built in the mid 1800's, we've been told it was the showcase of the North Country at the time. That was way back then.

By the time my husband Al's father purchased it in the '50's, it had been resold and also rented out quite a few times. It was by then, a total wreck.

Al's mother told me that her first impression of the place was not a good one.

A goat came running out of the house to greet her, chickens were running all over the downstairs and were on the kitchen table and flies were everywhere.

She said she actually had to scrape the once beautiful hardwood floors with a putty knife before she could scrub them. She hated the place!

On the other hand, Al's father loved it. He had finally purchased the farm he had always wanted.

To make a long story short, she left after enduring the place for several years.

Although Al maintained a relationship with her all through his childhood, he remained on the farm with his father.

After graduating from high school, he joined the Air Force and married his high school sweetheart. The union produced two beautiful little girls. In time they separated. She took the children and moved back into town and Al continued to stay here on the farm his father had left him.

Some years later I came into the picture.

It's been almost 30 years since then till now. For many years Al and I tried to restore some of the beauty this place once had. It's been years of hard work and determination from both of us. Now, when you drive to the end of this road, you can see the fruits of our labor.

This pretty old Victorian house seems (to outsiders) like the perfect place to live. Gorgeous trees, large green lawns and a number of outbuildings make for a lovely country setting. Wildlife abounds!

Quiet . . . . no neighbors on either side of the house and situated at the end of a newly paved road with nothing beyond but the woods. Traffic is virtually non-existent. Soft summer breezes, birds chirping . . . . How perfect could this all be?

I'M GOING TO TELL YOU!

Dead End

As the time nears for us to travel north to spend the summer in the old farmhouse, I'm filled with anticipation . . . . and dread.

Great thoughts of the many good times we spent there, watching our children, their growing up and our grand children. There were my beautiful flower gardens, great friends, going fishing, camping and just good memories. But all of these wonderful times are overshadowed by the uninvited and unwelcome house guest that lingers there.

You might think I would be able to put the unpleasant memories of past events behind me. Nine months out of each year spent in the sunny south helps . . . but . . . then it's time to return to the farm again for the summer.

Each year I like to think "Maybe it will be gone this time." "Maybe it got sick of not having anyone to harass during those long winters away and it moved on to greener pastures." But every year when I got there, reality sets in . . . . It's still there waiting. What was it plotting for me this year?

I guess you've noticed by now that I refer to my unwanted house guest as "IT". That's because I really don't know what else to call it.

Spirit, entity, poltergeist, spook, what? I don't even understand how it gets its power. How can something you can't "see" move things? How can it have physical contact? How can it whistle tunes?

The only good thing I can say about it is that it has never caused me any physical damage. Mental is debatable.

One thing for sure, I have never forgotten one of the many "occurrences" I've had with it over the span of the last 27 years.

Thirty years ago, if I had started to read a book like this, I would have slammed it shut right about here. I probably would have said "this is so much bull, how do they make up this crap?" That was 30 years ago. Now I'm here to tell you—if it can happen to me, it can happen to you.

You don't have to believe it. You do have to learn to live with it.

Let me start from the beginning:

I had only lived in the house for several months. It was in the early spring of the year and still nippy outside, windy, wet and muddy. The driveway was a virtual quagmire. There was no sidewalk leading to the house entrance and mud was tracked in constantly. The place was pretty much the same way on the outside as it had been when it was built way back in the late 1800's.

The inside wasn't much better. Windows that would not open unless you took off the wooden pieces that held them in, plaster falling off the walls in the hallway and some of the bedrooms upstairs, floors on slants because of all the years of the old house "settling", wallpaper (identified from the 40's) that was yellowing and peeling in spots in many of the rooms, rickety old stairs off the kitchen area led down to a muddy floor with planks that led to a washer and dryer that I was sure had come over on the Mayflower. The wood furnace was downstairs also. In order to keep the house somewhat warm, it had to be fed logs all day. They never lasted throughout the night and the house was very cold every morning. Over the years all of this has been rectified and the old place looks pretty good now.

The Footsteps

A s I mentioned, the house was built back in the late 1800's and the cellar wasn't finished. It had stone walls and a stone floor with mud. Of course that's where the washer and dryer were located. If you survived the creaky old stairs to get down to the cellar, you had to step on the wooden planks to stay out of the mud. I always managed to step off while loading the washer or furnace.

The door to the basement was a constant struggle. I could get it open partially, then have to force it the rest of the way to get through it. It seems like the old house had settled over the years and the floor had lifted there. When you wanted to shut it, you had to pull real hard to get it off the raised area.

Al needed to take the door off and shave the bottom of it off. Irritating as it was, the jobs still needed to be done. I forced the door open and descended the rickety old stairs with my basket of dirty clothes.

The washer and dryer in the basement were located directly below the kitchen door and I had just put the clothes in the washer when I heard the kitchen door open. Heavy footsteps came right to the basement door and slammed it shut. Of course I thought it was Al. What the Hell is he mad about, I thought. Because I left the basement door open?

I started the washer and went upstairs to see what was wrong. "Al" I called. No answer. I looked in all the downstairs' rooms. No Al. Thinking that he might have gone back outside, I looked out the kitchen window. No car. In fact, no new tire marks in the muddy driveway. What the Hell is going on here, I thought. Is someone trying to scare me? I checked the floor in the entrance room and the outside steps. No wet tracks. How could that be I thought. How could anyone have entered the house without leaving tracks?

Al came in about a half hour later. After I told him what had happened, he checked every room in the house. Nothing!

During dinner, I told Donna what had happened. She said "That happened to me too. I was taking a shower and had left the bathroom door open because I knew dad wouldn't be coming in that early." She heard the door open and the footsteps coming across the floor.

Grabbing a towel to wrap around her, she hurried and shut the bathroom door. After she was dressed, she looked around the house for her dad. He wasn't there.

Needless to say, we both agreed it was creepy. It was the topic of conversation around the house for a few days and then it kind of wore out as we busied ourselves with our daily routines.

The Fly Room

One of my first battles in this old house was to eliminate the flies. They were a constant annoyance.

Until I came here, I had never even heard of "cluster" flies. They live and breed in the walls of these old farmhouses. They come out of every crack and crevice and will form large clusters, usually in corners of rooms near the ceilings. It's an ugly sight and one I never want to see again.

Armed with a large can of fly spray, I was on a mission. I decided to start in the attic. The sun was out, the windows were warm and just loaded with flies. By the time I had finished spraying, the spray was running down the windows. I would clean it up later I thought as I descended the stairs to the next level. I felt pretty smug as I closed the door on them.

The second floor of the house has five bedrooms. Two were being used as bedrooms and the other three were stockpiled with what I called junk, Al considered it all treasures from the past.

The doors to these three rooms were always kept shut.

I started my spraying in the one small storage room at the top of the stairs. It was the worst room in the house for flies.

After spraying it thoroughly top to bottom, I closed the door as I left so none could escape. The sound of their dying, buzzing sounds was music to my ears.

I did the same in every room, taking particular aim at windows and ceiling corners. I closed each door as I left so they would be unable to escape the fumes. For the first time I realized that the rooms all went in a circle, just as they did downstairs, I thought it unusual. I recalled one time when I was young, going for a ride with my dad. We passed a house with a circular room. I asked my dad "why is that room round?" He said, "That's so the devil can't corner you." I'm still content with his answer.

As I started down the stairs, I heard buzzing sounds again coming from the room I sprayed first. It was full of flies again! I thoroughly re-sprayed the room again, taking particular delight in watching them spinning around on the floor as they were dying. Again I closed the door and went downstairs for a coffee break and fresh air. After my short break, I grabbed the vacuum cleaner and ascended the stairs. I couldn't believe it! I heard them before I even opened the door. On the floor hundreds of dead flies. On the windows and walls, a fresh army of them. I sprayed again, then left the room feeling thoroughly defeated.

Somehow I knew it was a battle I couldn't win.

A lot of years have passed since then. The old windows have been replaced with new ones and we have sealed every crack we could find in that room. Still they persist. Needless to say, the door always remains shut.

The Poke

I hated sleeping upstairs. It was so hot and stuffy up there in the summertime. The windows were so old and had been painted around so many times that in order to open them, you had to remove the framing. Then when we got them up, they wouldn't stay up without a support or they would stick and you had to force them down.

Expandable window screens never fit properly and every mosquito in Jefferson County knew it! The winters were even worse. It was so cold up there. All we had at the time was a wood burning stove, and it was downstairs. The stove pipe from it went up into one of the bedrooms, but it wasn't ours. I would shiver and shake myself to sleep at night, but it never seemed to bother Al. I guess he was conditioned to it after all those years in this house.

One cold winter night, after shaking myself into a stupor, I finally fell asleep. A poke in the back woke me up abruptly. I glanced over at Al thinking that was a hint but he was asleep with his back to me. I attributed it to either a dream or perhaps a nerve jumping. I drifted back off to sleep again but then another big poke in the back! This time, Al was not only turned away from me . . . but was snoring! What the heck is going on?

This happened repeatedly all night. By morning, I was dragging. Over breakfast, I told Al about it and he thought maybe I had a nerve jumping also. I accepted that as a reason, though I questioned why it didn't occur when I was awake also.

By bedtime that evening I was exhausted. It didn't take long to fall to sleep. It not only happened again, but repeatedly all night. I was like a zombie all the next day.

On the third night, I must have fallen to sleep immediately. This time, as soon as it woke me up, I grabbed my pillow and a blanket and went downstairs. I slept on the couch with my back tight against the back of it.

The next day we rearranged the room Al used as an office and put a bed in. My first night sleeping there was filled with anticipation of a recurrence happening again but it never did and I never slept upstairs again.

B.O.

L ife settled back into its regular routine of cleaning, cooking, gardening and babysitting grandchildren and a puppy I got from a neighbor.

She was a Beagle, Bassett hound mix and could howl like a Banshee.

I was going to name her Daisy but the minute Al held her it changed. He said "You ought to name her B.O. the way she stinks." From that day on she was called B.O. It didn't take them long at the vets to realize she would not come to "BO" nor would she go into a private room there without me.

Time slipped by again and thoughts of my two unpleasant experiences here were not forgotten, but were set back into my memory bank.

The only unusual thing I noticed was every once in awhile I could detect the sweet odor of pipe tobacco. Most of the time it happened upstairs. It never scared me. In fact, it was quite pleasant.

Still I wondered . . . had a man that smoked a pipe lived here once? I decided "IT" was a man.

One night I asked Al if his dad had smoked a pipe and he said that he hadn't. He said his grandfather had lived here also but had been killed in an automobile accident out by Tremains Corners. Al's mother was driving. She tried to take the curve to fast on a slippery road and didn't make it. She wasn't hurt and the car wasn't damaged but the old man (her father) hit his head. He never regained consciousness. Al didn't remember much about him as he was quite small when it happened.

When Al was about 8 years old, his mother left and never came back. Although he had contact with her from time to time, he was raised here by his father. In 1971 his dad became very ill with Acute Inflammation of the Pancreas. After a brief stay in the hospital he passed away. The house and land was left to Al and so the question of who had lived here that smoked a pipe was still on my mind. How many people had lived in this old house?

It was built between 1870 and 1880 and was once considered a North County showplace. Charles Potter was the first owner and builder followed by Oscar Lee and then Delbert Lee, Ralph Lee, a Mr. Bonney (Ducky), followed by Al's dad who purchased the property in 1949 and then finally Al after his dad's passing.

So the property had passed through 7 owners and approximately 75 years to destroy the place. It has been in constant repair since.

The question still stands . . . who smoked the pipe?

The Last Letter

A l worked late each night and therefore slept longer in the morning than I did. I called it my quiet time.

Time to reflect on yesterdays and to decide what major job had to be attended to today. Also to work on a new poem I was writing or write to my youngest son Bill. Bill was in the Army, living in Kansas. He was a prison guard at the Fort Leavenworth Prison and I worried about him. Horrible place!

I hadn't seen him for several years and was so excited that he was getting a leave and would be coming home soon. He planned to go hunting with his brother to get his first deer as we had herds of them here.

I was midway thru a letter to him when I heard it. A light tap, tap, tap behind me. I turned to see what it was. The fall before, I had set three dried, decorative gourds on top of the refrigerator. I watched in amazement as the two gourds on each side of the center one jumped up and down. One would go up and one down approximately 3 to 4 inches each time. The center one never moved.

We had an old refrigerator that needed to be replaced soon. When it was running I compared the sound to that of a thrashing machine. It wasn't running!

I tried to finish my letter but the persistent tapping kept up. By that time I had figured out that "IT" was having a little fun with me this morning.

I couldn't concentrate on my letter and was getting angrier as it continued. I can't even have some peaceful time to write to my son I thought. Finally in total disgust, I turned around and pointed my finger. Angrily I said, "I'm not paying attention to you anymore." No sooner had the words come out of my mouth when the gourds began to jump so high they almost hit the ceiling.

I must have ticked him off I thought. I never looked back again. I finished my letter and the tapping stopped.

Little did I know then, it would be my last letter to Bill. Shortly after, I was notified that he had been shot and killed. The days after that were a blur. Nothing was real. Our lives were devastated.

At the funeral, when they handed me the flag I remember thinking "I don't want a flag, I want my son."

Time went on . . . .

The Image

Staying busy helped but never eased my pain. One morning early, while having my wake up coffee, the door opened and in walked my son, Carl. He was carrying Bill's rifle. I should say Carl's rifle because Bill had given it to him before he went back to Fort Leavenworth the last time.

Carl informed me he was going out to get Bill's deer for him. He had a cup of coffee with me, set his Polaroid camera on the table and left. It wasn't long before he was back. "Mom" he said, "Will you help me hoist Bill's deer up in the tree?" It was a big one. Bill would have been so proud, I thought. I ran back to the house to get the camera.

Carl usually didn't like to have his picture taken but this day it was OK. We hurried back to the house to wait for the picture to come out. As it did, the tears welled up in my eyes. Carl said "Do you see what I see?" Yes, I did! When I took the picture I made sure to center Carl and the deer. It wasn't that way now.

The deer was in the center, Carl on the right side of it and a perfect image of a man on the left side.

Was this Bill's way of thanking his brother? Carl took the picture with him when he left and I never saw it again. I always thought it was a gift from God to help us heal our hearts. Several times over the last 23 years I asked about the picture but he has said the image faded out after awhile. I asked him again not long ago and he said he didn't remember. I do.

Fair Weather Friends

B.O. was full grown by now and was my constant companion. I couldn't even go to the bathroom without her.

Many nights when Al and I were watching TV, she would leave my side to go and stand in the doorway that led from the front room into the kitchen. She would stand and stare, then the bristles on her back would stand up and she would back up.

My comment to Al was always "IT's here." I could live with the knowledge that "IT" was scaring the crap out of my dog and giving me a break. To bad dogs can't talk . . . to bad some people can . . . me for instance.

I had confided in a gal I considered my friend about some of the events going on in this house. Apparently she told her husband and out of curiosity they dropped in unannounced one weekend. We invited them in and I put on a fresh pot of coffee.

We then all sat at the kitchen table gabbing. I tried several time to change the subject but they kept going back to questions about "IT". I really don't like to talk about "IT" in the house.

It seemed to me that his questions were made in a very snide manner. I tried to be a good sport about it, answering each question truthfully while ignoring his condescending attitude.

All of a sudden he jumped up out of his chair and said to his wife "Let's go." I asked what was wrong and he said he saw papers we had on the shelf, lift up and go back down. He said they would never come back in this house again and they never did.

I thought how does it feel to see something none of the rest of us was aware of?

I must admit I was as happy as a bedbug on a brand new Sealy. I said "Thank you" real low.

The Hall Of Horror

The largest bedroom upstairs has 4 large windows. The window on the left side of the room looks out upon the driveway and you can also see if anyone is driving down the dirt road. The window on the right side looks out at a field and wooded section.

The other two windows face the front of the house. You can see into the yard, my beautiful flower garden across the road and clear back to the woods.

It was my favorite room.

The afternoon sun would light the room up. The beds were almost always occupied by grandchildren. It was a happy room that dreadfully needed a face lift.

I used it for a sewing room also and on days I wasn't otherwise occupied, I would make stuffed toy and Raggedy Ann dolls for the children.

The door to the room faced out to a long hallway and Al and I had just finished putting a pretty floral wall paper there and painted all the trim. I was motivated! I decided first, the bedroom needed some new curtains. I picked out a pretty gingham material. It took me several days to make them as I wanted ruffles. Finally they were hung.

I stood back and admired them. Then I made a big mistake! I said (out loud), "Doesn't that look nice?"

I thought I heard something. I glanced down the hallway, nothing. Then I heard it again. Ha! I thought, Al must have snuck up the stairs to scare me. After all the times I had told him not to ever do that. I went over to the opposite door that leads into another bedroom. I thought I would see his shadow behind something, nothing. I crouched down and looked under the bed, nothing. That's when I got a real creepy feeling.

I stepped back over to the hallway door again. I couldn't see anything. Then I heard it!

As my memory goes back to that day, it's almost like reliving it again. That is something I never want to experience again. I'll do the best I can to describe the sound for you. Imagine a low, guttural, labored, breathing sound. Now imagine it getting louder and louder as it comes closer and closer to you. I was terrified!

I took a couple of steps backward. As I did I glanced out the window. **Al was down in the garden!**

To this day I don't recall if I ran through the other bedroom or actually ran through "IT" down the hallway. I'm not sure if my feet even hit the stairs. Next thing I knew I was in the garden crying and Al was hugging me. I told him what happened and that I was never going back in that house again. Naturally, as soon as I calmed down, we went back in together.

We searched every room thoroughly, nothing! Not a sound! To this day I will not go upstairs unless Al is in the house. I wish I could say it was all my imagination, but I can't forget the sounds. It upsets me to even write about it.

The Swinging Cups

I t was another cold, miserable winter day. Al had gone to work and I planned on working on crafts all day.

Before I had a chance to start, the phone rang. My sister-in-law, Connie, informed me that my mother had been in an automobile accident and had been transferred to the intensive care unit at the hospital. She told me my mother was asking for me.

I wondered why she would be asking for me. Maybe she wanted to make amends with me before she died. We hadn't spoken for years, so it was the only reason I could think of.

I'm sure my words must sound so cold to people reading this. I'm sorry for that. Possibly if they had endured the same childhood I did, they would be much more tolerant with me.

There were six of us children. All but the youngest were placed in foster homes very young or as a new born. Some of the places were nice, some not. Periodically we go back to live with our parents but it never lasted long. My mother had two favorite sayings, "I hate you kids" and "I wish you had never been born."

As for physical abuse, she could make Joan Crawford "Mother of the Year". Some things are better unsaid so I won't go any further with this.

My going to see her was quite a decision for me to make on such a short notice. Connie was waiting for my response. So many things went thru my mind. Would I feel guilty if she died and I hadn't made an attempt to see her? Would she be hateful and curse at me if I entered her room? I decided to take a chance and go.

On the way to the hospital I was processing the accident in my mind. No wonder, I thought, my mother was one of the world's worst drivers. Running red lights and stop signs was her forte' in life. She thought nothing of backing her car out of a parking place and scraping the one next to her all the way down its side. She would just drive away.

When I arrived at the hospital, my brother John met me and explained what had happened. Apparently she had pulled out of a gas station (probably without looking) directly into the path of an oncoming vehicle. The other driver couldn't stop on the icy highway. Both cars were totaled. The other driver escaped with bruises but she had gone through the windshield of her car and was thrown back in. She had to be removed with the "jaws of life" and suffered extensive bruising head to toe, a broken arm and her face was cut and imbedded with glass shards.

I was filled with apprehension as I entered her room. She looked at me, smiled and said my name. Must be some brain damage too, I thought. I approached her and held her hand. I told her how sorry I was that she had been hurt. We spoke for several minutes and she seemed so happy to see me, so docile—so not my mother! I left as she drifted off to sleep. They kept her in intensive care for several weeks.

My brother Tony and his wife Connie took her to their home when she was released. Mom was a very difficult person to live with. It had to be her way or the highway. After several weeks of enduring this, Connie called me and asked if I would take her for a few days. I told her I would, but if she got verbally or physically abusive with me or Al, she would be going back to them. We agreed.

Her bags were already packed and setting by the door when I arrived to pick her up. Connie couldn't have been happier as she bundled her up and helped her into the car. She had a big smile on her face as she waved goodbye to us. Her words to me were "Have fun." I was thinking "Oh God!"

After getting her home and settled in, I prepared a nice meal for us. We sat at the table after dinner and actually had a nice conversation. Then I got up to do the dishes.

I had my back to her when she asked "What's making them do that?" I looked at her and asked "What?" She pointed to the 4 coffee cups on a wooden peg board that hung on the wall. I was amazed to see that the two cups, one on each end, were swinging back and forth. The two in the center weren't moving. "I don't know, you tell me" was my response. As soon as I said it, the two that were swinging started moving up and down real fast. They actually swung to the tops of the pegs as if they were being juggled. After a minute or two they stopped. I was relieved that they didn't get broken as they were treasures to me. My son Billy had given them to me for Mother's Day, the year before he was killed. I explained to her that I didn't let these occurrences bother me anymore. She was visibly upset so I assured her it wasn't going to happen again.

The rest of the evening went quite well. As I was getting her ready for bed, she asked "Where am I going to sleep?" "Upstairs" was the only answer I could give. She gave me one of her looks—you know . . . the kind of look that would make a snake look for a rock to hide under. "If you think I'm going to sleep up there alone, you've got another think coming" she said. This . . . from a woman who was never afraid of anything? Wanting to pacify her, I said I would sleep up there also.

I did—until she fell asleep. My mother snored. In fact, she snored so loud we used to say she would wake the dead. I wasn't taking any chances. I crept down the squeaky old stairs and got into my own bed.

I'm not going to tell you what she called me when she came down in the morning. You can let your imagination run wild. There, I thought, is the mommy I remember.

While preparing breakfast for her she was giving me instructions on taking her back to my brothers. I called Connie and gave her the news. I must say she took it very graciously.

Lights Out

My sister comes to stay with us for a week or two every summer. We always have such a good time together. We spent our days checking out thrift shops, rummage sales and visiting relatives. At lunch time, we try to find a new place to eat every day.

At night we either watch TV or sit at the kitchen table and hash over new and old events in our lives. Naturally, the subject of "IT" always works its way into the conversation.

One summer she brought her daughter Linda with her. Linda was a quiet child and had always had been over protected by her mother (at least that was my opinion). She was a very naïve girl. Now in her mid teens, I didn't feel that we should omit her from our discussions. Not even the ones about "IT".

One night she was present as the subject was brought up. Other than interceding with an occasional "mommy!" She was very quiet. Bedtime came and as usual Carol said she hated to go up those stairs. Linda looked pretty scared but we both assured her that everything would be alright and that her mom would sleep with her. Content with that, Linda fell to sleep right away. Carol related to me the next morning that just as she started to drift off, she felt a hand on her shoulder. Adjusting her eyes to the darkness, she could see that Linda was sleeping with her back to her. After that she lay awake for a long time thinking it would happen again but it never did. I said "maybe "IT" realized it wasn't me and wasn't getting that much joy out of it.

The following year Carol brought her friend Bonnie and Bonnie's mother, with her. They were both from West Virginia, born and raised. The more the merrier. We had a ball—running around trying to show Bonnie's mother points of interest in the North Country. Her mom referred to it as "flat lands". Bonnie had been here before so she could come up with some interesting ideas too.

Saturday night was always our card playing night with friends. We had been doing it for years but we were willing to stay home with them if they wanted us to. They assured us they would be fine and to go and have some fun. Before we left, Carol asked me "What do I do if the lights go out?" I told her not to worry about that, they only went out during lightning storms.

On the way to our friend's house I said to Al "I'd love to sneak up into the attic while they're sleeping and make loud moaning sounds and drag a big chain across the floor." That to me was funny!

We got home quite late and found Carol still sitting at the kitchen table reading her "smut" magazines. She said she had been scared to death. Apparently, Bonnie and her mom had gone to bed and Carol decided to stay up and read. She said just as she started reading the lights went out. The house was in total darkness.

She made her way to the stairs by feeling things and hollered to Bonnie. Together they finally found the flashlight. Bonnie went downstairs into the cellar and found that the main breaker had shut off.

That had never happened before . . . nor since. One thing for sure—Carol would never have done it!

Here Kitty, Kitty

My sister Carol is a cat lover. Her cat, Squeeky had just passed away and she was broken hearted.

When Squeeky was born, his mother rejected him. Carol rescued him and fed him with an eye dropper and then a dolls bottle. He never did get to be very big but managed thru her love and devotion to live approximately 9 years. She lived so far away from me but I tried my best to console her over the telephone every night.

One day while leafing through a catalog, I saw a cute toy kitty. It looked so much like Squeeky. The ad said it mewed if you pressed it on the back of his neck. I decided to buy it and send it to her for Christmas. That was only two months away.

I was anxious for it to come so I could taunt my dog with it. If you even say "kitty", the dog would spaz. The package finally came and I hurried to open it, all the while saying "Here kitty, kitty." By the time I got it unwrapped, the dog was about to split a gut. I pressed the spot where it was supposed to make it meow. Nothing! I pressed it several more times. Nothing! By then I was more frustrated than the dog. Finally after several more futile attempts, I pressed it real hard. Meow, meow, meow—yeah! It worked! I had to put it up because by then the poor dog was in danger of having a total meltdown.

On top of the refrigerator seemed to be the safest place. I knew she couldn't reach it there.

Over the next several weeks, I showed it to everyone that stopped in. Each time, in order to get it to work, I had to press it very hard. Finally the novelty wore off and it was put up on the refrigerator again until Christmas time. I guess I forgot all about it.

Several weeks later, I was in the bathroom getting ready to go to the casino. I was in the process of putting on some makeup when I heard a cat crying. We have several barn cats. They aren't allowed in the house because I'm allergic to them. Naturally, my first thought was that one of them had come through the doggie door and into the house. I hurried out of the bathroom to catch the cat and get it out before the dog came back in.

To my surprise, the dog was already in. She was sitting in the kitchen looking up at the top of the refrigerator. Not barking, just staring. Just then another "meow, meow, meow". You guessed it! The cat on top of the refrigerator was the culprit. It was still meowing as I hurried out the door. Remembering just how hard it was for me to make it cry like that, motivated me to move a little faster. The dog was on its own.

I stayed away until I knew Al was home from work. Then the batteries were removed immediately, the cat was boxed and on its way to West Virginia early the next morning. It was way to early for Christmas and had no insurance on it but I didn't care.

Carol called and thanked me as soon as she received it. "You really have to press hard to make it meow, don't you?" She said. "They don't make things like they used to" was my answer.

Needless to say, it never meowed at Carol's house without being pressed . . . hard!

Prelude To The Whistler

My granddaughter Toni stopped in one afternoon unexpectedly. She said she couldn't stay more than an hour as she had to be back in Syracuse to work that evening.

We sat, drank coffee and gabbed for awhile. I excused myself to use the bathroom. I heard her say something just as I flushed the toilet but couldn't make out what it was.

When I came out of the bathroom I asked her "Did you say something to me?" "Yes, she said. "I asked you if you were whistling." "No...why?" I said. "Well somebody was" she said.

"Welcome to my nightmare" was my reply.

The Whistler

It was Saturday and Al's weekend to work long 10 P.M. to 10 A.M. shift. I hated being alone in this old house all night even though I had my two dogs "Maggie May" and "Bradey" to protect me.

Maggie was a mixed breed pound puppy and Bradey was an unusually large Saint Bernard I had purchased for Al one father's day. He wasn't fat. His nearly 280 pound body still had a lot of room to grow in. The vet said he was a freak. They were such a comfort to us after losing my constant companion "B.O." to cancer.

Saturday night was also the night I always drove to Syracuse to sell my craft items. I usually left about 9:00 P.M. and wouldn't get back home until 1 or 2 in the morning. Driving time usually took up to 3 hours of that time. Then I had to unload the car and put everything away again. If not, in the morning my kitchen looked like it had suffered a skud attack. That night I wanted to get it all picked up so I wouldn't disturb Al's sleep the next morning. I would be able to sleep later too.

We have a large back room off the kitchen. When I first came here it was a God awful mess. Al and his dad had used it for a work shop. I was told that in the 1800's it was used as a "summer kitchen". Over time Al had built himself a large work shop outside and moved most of the junk out there. It was now used as (you guessed it) a catch all for anything I didn't want in the house. Craft supplies, filing cabinets, food pantry, freezer and etc. He built some nice big shelves and it made all of my junk look neater. The room had 3 large windows and 3 doors in it. One door led to the kitchen, one outside door that opened to the side of the house and one to the woodshed and out into the back yard. It was a very large back yard that had been fenced in for the dogs. In the center of the room was a long craft table that was always loaded with sewing and craft items.

That night I had all of the windows open in that room and a nice breeze was coming in. I thought it was unusual that Bradey didn't follow me as I took the first box out there and Bradey always followed me but Maggie did instead.

I had just started to push the first box in on one of the higher shelves when I heard it. A distinct wolf whistle! With my arms still extended in the air, I froze. Then another whistle! I do know the difference between a whistle coming from a deer to that of one coming from a person. I stood in my frozen position as I heard it again.

By then, Maggie was running back and forth on the other side of the table with her nose to the floor and screaming. I've had many dogs in my lifetime and I have never heard a dog scream like that. Oh, my God, I thought. There's a man outside the window and the door is unlocked. I ran like my feet were on fire to the gun cabinet and grabbed a loaded rifle. Both dogs were right on my heels.

I was shaking like a leaf as I dialed 911 and told them there was a man in my yard. They said they would be there right away. With hands still shaking, I called Al and told him quickly what had happened. I knew he couldn't get off work until 10 A.M. when someone came in to relive him but that wasn't acceptable to me at the time.

The dogs and I (and the gun) went out on the entry porch and waited for the police to come. There were two of them, a man and a woman. She walked up to the door and he remained standing by their vehicle. She took one look in the door and saw Bradey and Maggie. "I don't do dogs" was her first comment to me. I really wanted to say "I don't do rude cops either" and slam the door in her face but I was terrified enough to keep my mouth shut.

I showed them how to go through the garage into the back yard, and waited. Armed with flashlights they left. A few minutes later they were back. I was informed that there were no tracks around the windows and the back yard was clear.

As they headed toward their vehicle, it hit me. No tracks in the yard? Maggie sniffing the floor and screaming? My God! It wasn't outside . . . "IT" was inside!

I was NOT staying here alone all night. I asked the police if they would wait for just one minute while I grabbed my purse and car keys so I could follow them out.

As I was at the end of our dead end dirt road, I was wondering where I could go at 3:00 in the morning. I certainly wasn't going to wake up any of my friends or family at that time in the morning. There were several all night diners in the area but I wasn't hungry as I had stopped and eaten on my way home from Syracuse. Ordinarily, a trip to the casino would be planned that night but all I had to spend was from my craft sales. I had planned on using it to restock on some of my sales. It didn't matter!

The casino was open all night and I had no intention of leaving it until daybreak. Needless to say, I donated my weekly profits to them. For once I didn't feel to bad about it. I figured it was worth every penny not to have to spend the night alone in the house. Did I say "alone?"

The Whistler Strikes Again

Al works nights at a government facility. Ordinarily he is home around midnight, but occasionally he has to work all night. I always have enough to do around the house to keep me busy. Days are usually spent doing housework and working on crafts. In the evening I enjoy watching TV or playing games on the internet.

One night, after finally giving up on trying to find something of interest to me on TV, I decided I would pass the rest of the evening playing games. After losing the first three games, I started picking up points and it looked like I was finally going to win one. I was totally absorbed in the game when I heard it.

Someone was whistling a tune behind me. I turned and looked. No one was there but the whistling continued. It seemed to be coming from the area where the door leads to the kitchen. I listened intently. La la la la la, la la la la la, over and over again. The tune sounded so familiar to me but I just couldn't think what it was.

I turned back to my game and started whistling along with "IT". I thought that would help me to remember the tune until Al got home. I guess that "IT" didn't like my whistling because he quit after I did it several times.

When Al came home I told him what had happened and asked him if he knew what the song was. I whistled it for him. La la la la la . . . la la la la la. "That's "Inchworm"" he said. Of course it was. I wondered then what "IT" meant by that song. Was he trying to say that he was "inching" up on me?

Whatever! I think I out did him on that one.

The New Doorbell

U p until several years ago, our entrance door was the same one they had installed when the house was built. I'm sure that in the 1800's it was a beautiful door. It had two elongated window panes in it that were full of air bubbles and all images seen through it were distorted. The old brass door lock with porcelain knobs was loose but still intact. To my knowledge, the key to it had been missing for umpteen hundred years, therefore it was always left unlocked.

It had a very decorative old bell on it that still worked. The problem was that the years had not been kind to the wood that surrounded all of the beautiful old treasures on it. The door had several large cracks in it that I would tell Al you could throw a cat through. When winter came, it might as well have not even been there for the cold air that came through it.

The day finally came when all of the years of my griping about it paid off. Al bought a pretty new door and installed it. I was satisfied . . . for awhile!

A new problem arose. In the summer when the air conditioning was running, you couldn't hear if someone knocked on it. In the winter, with the furnace running, it was the same thing.

I had friends telling me they had come to visit and had pounded on it and then left because they thought no one was home. Time to start griping again! Al went out and bought a new, wireless, door chime and installed it.

It didn't take long before it rang. I hurried to the door but no one was there. This happened several more times before I realized that "IT" had a new toy.

It rang mornings, afternoons, evenings and of course, in the middle of the night. When visitors came and it rang, they would say "Aren't you going to see who that is?" It was easier to tell them we had a short in the wiring than to explain why I ignored it.

"IT" was having a ball! Until I finally got sick of being woke up 3 to 4 times a night and took the batteries out. Now, until "IT" figures out how to replace the batteries, he can put his finger somewhere else.

What The Hell Was That?

My back has always been screwed up. I was born with scoliosis of the spine. Over the years, several of the discs in my lower back have deteriorated. Sometimes just a wrong movement can cause me to suffer long bouts of Sciatica in one or the other of my legs.

Now, older, I am the proud owner of osteoporosis. Have I mentioned rheumatoid arthritis or the spur at the top of my spine in the neck area? Anyway, operations for me are out of the question. Specialists tell me I am a poor risk. Movements that are quite normal to most others are very difficult for me. Such as, turning over in bed, that is always such a feat. Others turn, I flip.

For years it was the sofa for me. It was a place where I could get my back up against something firm. Also, not wide enough to allow me to get in my (used to be) favorite position, on my stomach. You want to talk about pain? I can't even walk in the morning if I do that.

I'm a smoker! I've been smoking for over 55 years and am not about to put them down for anyone . . . not even me. Begging, intimidation and lectures all fall on deaf ears with me. I enjoy them.

Because of this my lungs are ruined. It came to a point where I could not sleep laying down anymore. My lungs would fill and I would cough all night. Al bought me a beautiful recliner and I sleep in a partial, sitting up position now. It has helped a lot.

One night I had been in and out of sleep several times and flipping over each time. Ordinarily I don't even bother opening my eyes when I do that. This time I did.

I saw it come out of the kitchen into the front room, take a sharp turn and go into Al's room. It was a bright yellow, neon light that was very small and round in shape. It was moving very fast and left a trail of neon zig zag light behind it as it passed over the coffee table. It was about 3-1/2 feet high from the floor.

I said "What in the Hell was that" and fell back to sleep. I guess my attitude is different than most people after all I have experienced in this house during the last 25 years.

In the morning while drinking my coffee, I tried to rationalize the event. I'm aware that several medical ailments can cause you to have spots before your eyes or zig zags. Been there, done that! This was so different. I'll probably never know what it was but unlike everything else that has happened to me in this house . . . I wish I could see it again!

Phew

The first time it happened, Al and I were having our morning coffee and talking. Right in the middle of a sentence, he started to fan the air around him and said "Whew, did you smell that?" It's rotten! I was sitting across the table from him and I didn't smell anything. Several minutes later he said "There it is again," "What the Hell is that?"

Again, I couldn't smell anything. The third time it happened he said "Smell over here by me". I did! It was putrid! To this day we can't define the odor. We've compared it to dead fish, rotting garbage, raw sewage and many other things. I guess the dead fish would be the closest guess . . . . but much stronger. It would gag a maggot!

Each episode lasted only a short while and he would say "It's gone". We were talking about what it could be and trying to rationalize the event when it happened. It was right in my face! This time Al couldn't smell it. It happened several times and then was gone. We discussed it for awhile and not being able to come up with a reasonable answer for it, we set about our daily tasks.

The rest of the day went well and the event was forgotten. Until the next morning, that is. It happened again! It became an everyday, coffee time experience.

We searched the house from the attic to the basement trying to find a logical reason for it. Nothing we could see or smell anywhere and yet it persisted every morning. One morning, after several sickening bouts with it . . . I said to Al, "I don't know what it is, but whatever it is . . . it isn't alive!"

That did it! Al was headed to his computer to research the paranormal. After reading all he could about that, he went into a program on ghost hunters. He found and wrote to a woman claiming to be one. She didn't live that far away from us so he set up an appointment for her to visit our home.

Several years prior to this, we had talked with a preacher from a local church and he said he would help us. Upon arrival at our home he was more interested in our antiques and trying to get us to join his church, than he was in helping to rid us of "IT".

Of course, this left me very skeptical. Nevertheless, our ghost hunter arrived at the appropriate time set, with another woman. Supposedly another hunter! We did our best to explain to them some of the occurrences we had to endure in this house.

Solving the mystery of the horrible smell was our first priority at the time though. I kept hoping it would happen to them while we were talking, so I could see them gag.

They not only did not impress me, nor did I believe anything they said. Her theory on the whole situation was that it was a woman (huh?). She claimed that if we would start talking to it, while taping the conversation, that she would be able to detect any background voices. We agreed to try it.

We were grasping at straws . . . anything that would help us to rid the house of "IT" would be worth trying. We taped each morning and sent the tapes to her. Several months later, after not getting a response, we called her. She claimed they had been able to make out words like "Wouldn't you come in" and "I love you Beth." She said she had more work to do on the tape and that she would get back us when it was completed. That was several years ago now.

Christmas was such a delightful event that year. Donna and her boyfriend had come all the way from New Jersey to share it with us. It was the first time in many years that we had her home for the holiday. To top it off, my granddaughter, Toni, showed up too with her daughter Iris. Toni and Donna hadn't seen each other for many years and were happily rehashing the old days.

We were all standing by the kitchen table opening our gifts when it happened. From one of us to the next, the putrid smell hit. Even little Iris got a whiff.

Was it being curious about what was going on, or was "IT" just trying to upset our joyful reunion? I'll never know.

Life went on . . . as did the smell.

On another occasion, two other couples had come over and were all sitting at the kitchen table when . . . yep . . . Al got the first whiff and then the odor went around the table to each individual. As soon as it went to the next individual, the odor completely left the last individual. It went to everyone at the table as if inspecting them or trying to figure out who was next???? As soon as it made the round of the table, the odor was gone again . . . for awhile.

Al and I liked to go camping and fishing when we could. Quite often we would go to the Whetstone Gulf camping area. They had great facilities and nice camp sites. On more than one occasion after Al had the pop-up camper all set up and we had settled in for lunch and a little relaxation, Al would say "IT'S HERE". Evidently it had the ability to follow us on three of our camping trips and even on two occasions to North Carolina.

There was no mistaking the odor so it couldn't be confused with anything else. Maybe that was the reason, there would be no mistake!

Carl's Angel?

We hadn't seen Al's niece Kris for many years. She had lived with us for awhile as a teenager, then left to live with her Aunt in New Jersey.

She completed school there and went on to become a nurse. We were very proud of her. Eventually she married, move to Oregon, and had a little boy named Carl. Although we had received pictures of him periodically, we had never actually seen him. He was four years old now, they were coming to visit and we were very excited about it.

At long last, we were going to see Kris and meet Carl. I was hugging Kris as she came through the kitchen door and looking down at the cutest little blond haired boy. I knelt down and said "So this is Carl."

Before I even got a chance to hug him, he broke away and ran to the window. He was hollering "What's that?" We all ran to the window to see what he was so excited about. We didn't see anything. "Where" we asked him. "There, under the tree, a person" he said. He was so excited.

Then, as if nothing had happened, he walked away from the window. Kris said "He must have seen something Aunt June because Carl doesn't lie." I asked him if it was a man and he said "No, it was a woman."

My curiosity was at its highest peak then. I said "Carl, did she look like this?" and sketched a quick drawing of a woman. He said "No, that's a pirate." "She had long hair and wings—I drew it. "No," he said "She had big wings." Again I made a rough sketch. "Yes," he said, "Wings like that but her dress was long." I sketched it again with a long dress. "Yes" he said, "That's her." He was satisfied that his Great Aunt had been able to draw what he had seen (even if it was very crude).

It was the topic of conversation after that. When they left, Kris's parting words "We're coming back again next year. I want to see if he sees something else."

I was thinking "If that really was an angel, I wish it would come in and help us to rid this house of "IT"."

Holding Hands

For quite some time, my granddaughter Toni and I had discussed getting together for a little quality time. She and her little daughter, Iris lived approximately sixty miles away from us. Quite often our plans of getting together would be thwarted for one reason or another. The weather would be to nasty, she had to work or her old car would be on the fritz again.

Finally, after several months of careful planning, the circumstances were right and they were coming. I had made plans for the perfect evening. Toni's favorite meal was macaroni and cheese. I made it and a meat loaf then hurried over to the movie store and rented "Gone with the Wind". It's my favorite all time movie and Toni had never seen it.

Although it was a four hour movie, we both felt that Iris would watch it for awhile and then fall asleep. After they arrived, we had our dinner, sat and gabbed for awhile then retired to the living room. I made the sofa up for Iris to sleep on then I sat in the recliner and Toni sat in the rocker.

Iris was very good for the first two hours of the movie. A few questions and a trip to the bathroom was acceptable. During the intermission, I made some popcorn and a fresh pot of coffee. On going back into the living room, I found that Iris had claimed my chair. Toni told her to let me have my chair back but I reminded her how she used to do the same thing when she was little.

With that resolved, I headed for my new spot on the sofa and the movie resumed. I figured "Iris" wasn't going to last much longer anyway. After about 15 minutes, I glanced over to see if she had drifted off yet. I was amazed to see that she was still watching the movie intently with her right arm extended straight up in the air with her hand closed.

She must have sensed that I was looking at her because she glanced back. Then she looked at her mother with the most astonished look on her face. She said "Who's holding my hand? I thought it was you mommy." Toni looked at me in despair. "Grandma" she said. Quickly I told Iris "It's my guardian angel honey. She's watching over you to protect you."

I shot Toni a look that meant don't scare her. It was hard to concentrate on the movie after that, but Iris seemed very content to continue watching while holding hands with "IT".

After about fifteen more minutes of this, Iris started to nod off . . . hand still extended in the air.

We tucked her into bed on the sofa. Toni looked like she was in shock. We still said nothing. Iris fell to sleep almost instantly, with her arm still extended in the air. Toni finally voiced the words "My God, "IT's" touching my child. Grandma!"

"She believes it's a special angel Toni, so let's not ever tell her otherwise" I said. And so the evening ended. Iris content she had a special angel . . . Toni with a secret to keep . . . and I wanting to kick the crap out of a ghost.

Although this may be the last page of my book,
I sincerely doubt it will be the final chapter.
I never know when, or in what area of the house "IT"
will give me a new story to tell.
It's been very calm around here for over a month . . . I'm waiting!
So is "IT".

If anything good has come from sharing our home with "IT" . . .
it's that I don't have to endure these episodes on a daily basis.
I do live every day with the anticipation of what "IT's" next trick will be.
I'm sure it will be a good one!

About The Author

I regret to say that June Marie Lawrence passed away February 12, 2013. She started this book in 1995 but was reluctant to finish it until she was encouraged by family and friends.

Before she passed she requested that I finish it and get it published and I told her I would. It would be the last thing that I could do for her.

Rest easy Sweetheart

Printed in the United States
By Bookmasters